WHAT IF a Stranger Approaches You?

by Anara Guard

illustrated by Colleen M. Madden

PICTURE WINDOW BOOKS
a capstone imprint

WITHDRAWN

Thanks to our adviser for his expertise and advice:
Terry Flaherty, PhD
Professor of English
Minnesota State University, Mankato

Editor: Shelly Lyons
Designer: Ashlee Suker
Art Director: Nathan Gassman
Production Specialist: Sarah Bennett
The illustrations in this book were created digitally.

Picture Window Books
1710 Roe Crest Drive
North Mankato, MN 56003
www.capstonepub.com

All books published by Picture Window Books
are manufactured with paper containing at least
10 percent post-consumer waste.

Library of Congress Cataloging-in-Publication Data
Guard, Anara.
  What if a stranger approaches you? / by Anara Guard;
illustrated by Colleen M. Madden.
    p. cm. — (Danger zone)
  Includes index.
ISBN 978-1-4048-6683-6 (library binding)
ISBN 978-1-4048-7031-4 (paperback)
 1. Children and strangers—Juvenile literature.
2. Safety education—Juvenile literature.
3. Kidnapping—Prevention—Juvenile
literature. 4. Crime prevention—Juvenile literature.
I. Title.
  HQ784.S8G83 2012
  613.6083—dc22   2011006988

Printed in the United States of America
in North Mankato, Minnesota.
122011   006506R

A stranger is a grown-up or teenager you haven't met before. Most people are kind to children. But some strangers are not nice, even if they seem kind.

The stories and tips in this book will help you learn how to be safe. They will also help you know when there might be danger.

What If a Stranger Wants to Talk to You?

Mary and her friends are playing in the park. Mary chases after the ball.

A woman on a park bench asks her questions.

Mary doesn't want to talk with her. She runs back to her friends.

SAFETY TIP

Don't talk to strangers! If a stranger makes you feel uncomfortable, it's OK not to talk to him or her.

5

What If a Stranger Wants to Give You Treats or Presents?

Lucy waits for her mom to pick her up.

A man comes out of the school and asks, "Would you like a soda?"

Lucy wants the soda, but she says, "No!" She tells her mom about it right away.

SAFETY TIP

Ask first! Before taking anything from a stranger, ask your parents.

What If a Stranger Asks You For Help?

A man leans over Sarah's fence. He says, "I lost my puppy. Will you help me find him?"

Sarah says, "No!" Then she runs inside to tell her mom.

SAFETY TIP

Check in! Ask your parents before helping a stranger.

What If a Stranger Knows Your Name?

Mark hears a man calling to him.

The man yells, "Mark, why don't you come over here?"

Mark goes into the library. When his dad comes, Mark tells him everything.

11

What If a Stranger Comes Near You?

At the playground, a man offers to push David on the swing.

David doesn't feel right about it. He says, "No!" Then he runs back to his babysitter.

SAFETY TIP

No unwanted touches! If someone makes you feel uncomfortable, run away. Then tell your parents or a trusted adult.

What If a Stranger Wants You to Go Somewhere?

On the way home from school,
Joe sees a car pull up near him.

The driver says, "Your mom
sent me to give you a ride home."

SAFETY TIP

Don't take a ride! Always ask your parents before taking a ride from anyone.

Joe backs up and yells, "No!" He runs away and calls his dad.

At home, Joe and his parents talk about what to do.

His dad says, "If we ever send someone to pick you up, we will give him a password."

"What's a password?" asks Joe.

"A secret code that only you, Mom, and I know. Let's pick one together. We will use the password only if we need it."

SAFETY TIP
Choose a password! And don't tell anyone else what the code word is.

What If Your Friends Want You to Do Something Unsafe?

Rita, Kenny, Chris, and Ava always walk to school together.

One morning Kenny is worried they will be late. "Let's take this shortcut," he says.

Rita says, "We have to ask a trusted adult first."

"I'll go by myself," says Kenny.

Chris says, "We need to stick together. Let's stay safe."

"You're right," says Kenny. "But let's hurry!"

SAFETY TIP

Stick with your friends! Never go anywhere alone.

Talk with your family about how to be safe around strangers. It is always a good idea to tell grown-ups you trust—your mom and dad, your teacher, your babysitter—if you feel scared or uncomfortable around other people. Remember these tips:

- Don't talk to strangers!

- Ask first! Always ask your parents before you take food or gifts from someone.

- Check in! If a stranger asks you for help, check with your parents to see if it's OK.

- Don't wear your name! Don't wear clothing or backpacks that show your name.

- No unwanted touches! If someone makes you feel uncomfortable, run away and tell a trusted adult.

- Don't take a ride! If a stranger offers you a ride, ask your parents first.

- Choose a password! Create a code word with your family that can be used when needed.

- Stick with your friends! In public places, stay near family or friends.

Role-Playing

Play this game with your parents or a trusted adult. When they ask you the question, answer with the correct words or actions.

- ◻ What if you are walking home from school and an adult says he wants help finding his dog?

  Answer: Yell, "No!" Then run and tell a trusted adult.

- ◻ What if a stranger wants to take your picture?

  Answer: Yell, "No!" Then run and tell a trusted adult.

- ◻ What if your friend wants you to do something dangerous?

  Answer: Tell your friend, "No." Then stick to what is safe.

- ◻ What if it is very cold outside and your friend's mother asks you if you want a ride?

  Answer: If your friend's mother knows the code word, you can take a ride. If not, go find a trusted adult.

- ◻ What if a stranger wants to show you something in his or her car?

  Answer: Yell, "No!" Then run and tell a trusted adult.

GLOSSARY

password—a word that you and your family agree on as a secret code; Only someone who knows the password can give you a ride

shortcut—a shorter route

stranger—a person older than you who you don't know

trusted adult—an adult you know and can talk to

MORE BOOKS TO READ

Denshire, Jayne. *Safety*. Healthy Habits. Mankato, Minn.: Smart Apple Media, 2011.

Johnson, Jinny. *Being Safe*. Now We Know About. New York: Crabtree Pub. Company, 2010.

Rissman, Rebecca. *We Can Stay Safe*. Chicago: Heinemann Library, 2010.

INTERNET SITES

FactHound offers a safe, fun way to find Internet sites related to this book. All of the sites on FactHound have been researched by our staff.

Here's all you do:

Visit *www.facthound.com*

Type in this code: 9781404866836

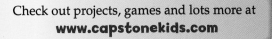

Super-cool stuff!   Check out projects, games and lots more at
www.capstonekids.com

ABOUT THE AUTHOR

Anara Guard is a short story writer and poet who has worked in the field of injury prevention since 1993. She speaks around the country on a variety of topics related to unintentional and intentional injury. For seven years, she worked for the Children's Safety Network, a national injury and violence prevention resource center. Ms. Guard has also been a parent educator and a librarian. She has a master's degree in library and information science and a certificate in maternal and child health. The mother of two grown sons, she lives and writes in California.

INDEX